Jerusalem Recipes

A Cookbook of Israeli and Arab Traditions

Encore Book Club

Fabulous Free eBook Cookbooks Every Week!

Our eBooks are FREE for the first few days of most publications. You will be the first to know when new books are published. We frequently offer exclusive promotions. Our collection includes hundreds of books that on a wide variety of topics including healthy foods, diets, food allergy alternatives, gourmet meals, desserts, and easy and inexpensive meals.

Sign-up at:
www.encorebookclub.com

View a complete list of our
Best Selling Recipe Book Series:
www.encorebookclub.com/booklist

Table of Contents

Breakfast

Yemeni Shakshouka

Prep time: 10 minutes
Cooking time: 20 minutes
Servings: 2-3 persons

Ingredients

- 5 eggs
- 3 plum tomatoes, chopped
- 1 onion, chopped
- 1 green chili
- ½ tsp hawaij spice mixture
- 2tbs oil
- Salt to taste
- Ground black pepper

Directions

1. Add oil to a pan and heat, put in the onions, salt, and chili, fry until the onions are golden, about 4-5 minutes.
2. Drop in the tomatoes, pepper, and hawaij, cook for 5 minutes.
3. Whisk the eggs, and put in the tomatoes, cook for 3minutes, give it a mix, making sure it is cooked evenly.
4. Dish up with tea, and bread.

Susi (Fattah)

Prep time: minutes
Cooking time: minutes
Servings: persons

Ingredients

- 2 medium flat breads
- 3 eggs
- ¼ cup butter, melted
- 1⅔ cups of milk
- Black sesame seeds
- Salt to taste

Directions

1. Heat the stove to 400°F.
2. Spray grease a baking dish and lay in the broken bread.
3. Whisk the eggs together and add the milk, mix well.
4. Now add the salt and 2 tablespoons dissolved butter.
5. Pour the mix over the bread and let it soak in for 5 minutes.
6. Add a little extra milk if it becomes too dry.
7. Dust the seeds over and place in the oven for 20 minutes.
8. Finish under the broiler to color the top.
9. Take out and remove the excess butter.
10. Other ingredients can be added, like dates, banana, or even meat.

Shakshuka

Prep time: 25 minutes
Cooking time: 60 minutes
Servings: 4-6 persons

Ingredients

- 7 cloves garlic, chopped finely
- 3 tablespoons canola oil
- ¼ cup tomato paste
- 1 ½ tablespoons kosher salt
- 2 medium yellow onions, diced
- 1 tablespoon ground cumin
- 1 large jalapeno pepper, deseeded and diced
- 1 teaspoon ground caraway
- 8-12 large eggs
- 1 green bell pepper, deseeded and diced
- 1 tablespoon sweet paprika
- 1 – 28 ounce can whole peeled tomatoes, crushed
- 2 ½ tablespoons sugar
- ½ bunch Swiss chard or spinach, trimmed and chopped
- 1 bay leaf
- 1 ½ teaspoons black pepper

Directions

1. Add the oil to a frying pan and heat, once hot add the onions and fry for 5-6 minutes.
2. Next put in the two kinds of peppers and cook for a further 4 minutes.
3. Now add the tomato paste with the garlic and cook for 2 minutes more.
4. Now stir in the crushed tomatoes, bay leaf, cumin, sugar, pepper, caraway, salt and paprika, cook for 20 minutes.
5. Lay the spinach or Swiss chard on top.
6. Add the eggs to the tomato mix, place a lid on and let it cook for another 10 minutes to cook the eggs.
7. Dish up.

Masoob, Masoub, Malikia

Prep time: 10 minutes
Cooking time: 0 minutes
Servings: 2-3 persons

Ingredients

- 3-4 bananas, over ripe
- 1 tablespoon fresh cream
- 2-3 flatbreads
- 2 teaspoon honey
- 10-15 sliced almonds
- ¼ cup milk
- 1 tablespoon raisins or dates

Directions

1. Take the bananas and peel them, then mash them using a fork or even in the blender, and put to one side.
2. Next add the flatbread to the blender or grinder, now mix together with the banana, it should be 50/50 mix, if it is too thick add some milk.
3. Mold the mix into shape and place in the serving dish.
4. Drop the almonds, raisins on top then spoon over the honey and cream.
5. Place in the microwave for 30 seconds, this is up to you if you want hot or cold.
6. Enjoy.

Shakshuka, Champions Breakfast

Prep time: 25 minutes
Cooking time: 60 minutes
Servings: 4-6 persons

Ingredients

- 1 large green bell pepper, sliced, deseeded and diced
- 7 cloves garlic, chopped fine
- 2 ½ tablespoons sugar
- 3 tablespoons canola oil
- 1 ½ tablespoons kosher salt
- 2 medium yellow onions, diced
- 1 bay leaf
- 1 teaspoon ground caraway
- 8-12 large eggs
- 1 tablespoon cumin
- ¼ cup tomato paste
- 1 tablespoon Hungarian paprika
- 1 – 28 ounce can whole peeled tomatoes
- 1 ½ teaspoon ground black pepper
- ½ bunch Swiss chard or spinach, trimmed and chopped
- 1 large jalapeno, deseeded and diced

Directions

1. Add the oil to a frying pan and heat.
2. Once hot fry the onions for 5-7 minutes
3. Next add the jalapenos and bell peppers cook for 4 minutes further.
4. Add the tomato paste and mix in the garlic frying for a further 2 minutes.
5. Now stir in the rest of the ingredients apart from the Swiss chard and eggs.
6. Cook together for 20 minutes, then lay the leaves over the top.
7. Break the eggs in the mix and place a lid on for 10 minutes.
8. Once the whites are cooked dish up.

Shakshuka with Fennel and Feta

Prep time: 20 minutes
Cooking time: 30 minutes
Servings: 6 persons

Ingredients

- 1 small onion, diced
- 1 green bell pepper, diced
- 2 tablespoons extra virgin olive oil
- 1 tablespoon harissa
- 1 jalapeno, seeded and diced fine
- 6 large eggs
- 1 small fennel bulb, cored and sliced thin
- 2 tablespoons chopped parsley
- Kosher salt
- 1 teaspoon Spanish paprika
- ½ cup water
- ½ cup feta cheese crumbled
- 1 – 28 ounce can whole tomatoes, chopped
- 2 serrano chilies, seeded and chopped
- 2 cloves garlic, minced

Directions

1. Add the oil to a frying pan, once hot fry the fennel with the onion for 3 minutes, until tender.
2. Next add the bell pepper and both chilies, season and cook for a further 6-8 minutes, before adding the paprika, harissa and garlic.
3. After 1 minute add the water and tomatoes, simmer for 10 minutes.
4. Break the eggs on top of the sauce, place the lid on and cook until the eggs are done, keeping the yolk soft.
5. Add the sauce with the eggs into the serving bowls and finish with the feta and parsley.

Israeli Salad

Prep time: minutes
Cooking time: minutes
Servings: 2-4 persons

Ingredients

- 2 large tomatoes
- 3 medium cucumbers, if English you only need 1
- 1 green or red bell pepper
- For the dressing
- Salt to taste
- Olive oil
- Black pepper to taste
- 1 lemon, juiced

Directions

1. Dice the tomatoes, peppers and cucumber, place in a bowl.
2. Mix in the juice and oil with the seasoning as you are about to serve.
3. If desired you can add chopped mint, ¼ red onion diced fine or scallions diced fine for extra flavor, even feta cheese.

Egg and Cheese Bread, Kale Khachapuri

Prep time: 60 minutes
Cooking time: 20 minutes
Servings: 2-4 persons

Ingredients

- 1 tablespoon olive oil
- 1 teaspoon active dry yeast
- 2 cups muenster cheese, grated
- ¼ teaspoon granulated sugar
- 2 eggs
- 1 ½ cups kale, chopped
- 1 teaspoon kosher salt
- 1 cup ricottas cheese, crumbled
- 1 ¼ cups all-purpose flour
- 4 tablespoons unsalted butter, diced

Directions

1. Mix the sugar, yeast and 2/3 cup of warm water together and rest it for 10 minutes.
2. Once it becomes foamy add 1 teaspoon salt, flour, and 1 tablespoon of oil, stir this into a dough mix.
3. Flour a work top and knead the dough until it becomes smooth, this usually takes 4 minutes.
4. Now allow it to rise.
5. Meanwhile add 1 tablespoon of oil to skillet and fry the kale until tender, then add the 2 types of cheeses and season, mix well.
6. When the dough is ready, knock it back and split into 2, make each piece into an oval shape rolling out to about 1/8 inch thick.
7. Smear half the mix, leaving the edge clear.
8. Then roll the edge towards the mix and repeat on the other side, seal the two ends to form a boat shape then do the same with the other half.
9. Place the two boats onto a lined baking tray and cook in the oven for 15 minutes, now break an egg in the middle of each one and bake again for 4-5 minutes until the egg white has set.
10. Dish up.

Main Dishes

Lahma Mahshoosha
Prep time: 15 minutes
Cooking time: 35 minutes
Servings: 6-8 persons

Ingredients
- 4 pounds' beef, place the fat on one side
- ¼ cup butter, if there is no fat on the beef
- 7 cloves garlic, minced
- 1 large onion, diced
- 1 teaspoon salt
- 1 tablespoon ground cumin
- 1 teaspoon coriander
- 1 teaspoon ground black pepper
- ½ teaspoon turmeric
- ⅛ teaspoon cinnamon
- Pinch cloves
- Cardamom

Directions
1. Trim the meat and keep the fat on one side.
2. Dice the meat beef into cubes, and heat the butter or beef fat in a pressure cooker or pot.
3. Once hot add the meat, garlic and onions with the spices and salt.
4. Place the lid on and cook, 20 minutes for the pressure cooker or 60 minutes for a pot.
5. If you are using a pot you may have to top up the liquid and stir so it does not stick to the base.
6. Once the beef is soft, take out and place under a broiler to brown, but do not burn it.
7. Slightly reduce the broth to get more flavor and you do not want the beef swimming, it should be a little dry.
8. Serve up together.

Syrian Meat Pie (Safiha)

Prep time: 120 minutes
Cooking time: 15 minutes
Serving: 6 persons

Ingredients

- For the dough
- 3 ½ cups of flour
- 2 ½ cups of yeast
- 1 teaspoon salt
- 1 teaspoon sugar
- 1 teaspoon olive oil
- For the filling
- 1-pound ground meat
- 1 teaspoon pomegranate syrup
- 1 teaspoon salt
- 1 medium onion, minced
- ¼ teaspoon black pepper
- ⅓ cup raw pine nuts
- ½ teaspoon saffron
- ½ cup thick yogurt
- ½ teaspoon allspice

Directions

1. Place the sugar with the yeast together in ½ cup of warm water and leave for 5 minutes.
2. In a large bowl mix the flour with the salt.
3. Next slowly add the yeast to it along with the ¾ cup warm water and the oil, blend together using your clean hands.
4. Rest the dough for 1-2 hours covered.
5. Pre-heat the stove to 475°F.
6. Now knock the dough back and divide into 6, mold them into rounds like pizza bases and rest for a further 30 minutes.
7. Place on a baking tray.
8. Now make the filling, blend together the meat, pine nuts, onions and spices, along with the saffron and seasoning, mix well.
9. At the end add the pomegranate syrup and yogurt.
10. Spoon the mix over the bread evenly.
11. Cook for 15 minutes.
12. When ready dish with some yogurt.

Cypriot Taro Casserole

Prep time: 15 minutes
Cooking time: 50 minutes
Servings: 4-6 persons

Ingredients

- 3 tablespoons olive oil
- 1 ¼ pounds chicken pieces, diced, bone and skinless
- 2 tablespoons tomato paste
- 1 large onion, diced
- ¾ pound prepared taro root
- 2 cups chicken stock
- 1 lemon, juiced
- Salt to taste
- Black pepper to taste
- 1 – 16 ounce can diced tomatoes

Directions

1. Add 1/3rd of the oil to a frying pan, once hot place the chicken in and seal all over until golden brown, add to a casserole dish.
2. Next put 1/3rd of the oil in the same pan and fry the taro until golden, once done add to a second casserole dish.
3. Put the remaining oil in the pan and fry the onions, add the chicken back in and mix together.
4. Blend in the tomato paste, stock and diced tomatoes, reduce the heat until it simmers.
5. Add in the taro, seasoning and lemon juice, cook for 30 minutes.
6. Add more stock if required.
7. Dish up with bread, salad or pilaf rice.

Spinach and Feta Borek

Prep time: 200 minutes
Cooking time: 20 minutes
Servings: 3-4 persons

Ingredients

- 7 sheets phyllo pastry
- ½ cup skimmed milk
- Pinch of salt
- 2-3 tablespoons olive oil
- 2 medium eggs
- For the filling
- 1 brown onion, grated
- ¾ pound frozen spinach
- 1 tablespoon olive oil
- Seasoning to taste
- ⅓ cup feta cheese, crumbled

Ingredients

- Take the filling ingredients and fry the onions for 5 minutes, then stir in the spinach with the seasoning and cook for 2 minutes.
- Take off the heat and blend in the feta, put to one side.
- Whisk the milk, eggs and oil together in a bowl.
- Grease a casserole dish with spray oil and lay 2 sheets of the pastry on the base and sides.
- Next smear with egg wash and add another 2 sheets folded, covering the base only and egg wash.
- Evenly spread the spinach on the base and lay another 2 sheets to cover with egg wash.
- Use the rest of the pastry each time using egg wash, when finished fold over the sides.
- Pre-heat the stove to 350°F, while the pastry is resting in the fridge for 2 hours.
- Take out and cook for in the oven until golden all over.
- Take out cool and slice, dish up.

Spinach Salad with Dates and Almonds

Prep time: 10 minutes
Cooking time: 10 minutes
Servings: 2 persons

Ingredients

- ½ medium red onion, sliced thin
- Salt to taste
- ½ cup whole unsalted almonds
- 1 tablespoon wine vinegar
- 2 tablespoons butter, unsalted
- 3 ½ ounces dates, pitted and cut in 4
- 2 tablespoons olive oil, divided
- ½ teaspoon chili flakes
- 5-6 ounces' baby spinach
- 2 teaspoons sumac
- 2 small pitas
- 2 tablespoons fresh lemon juice

Directions

1. Add the dates, vinegar and onions to a bowl, add a little salt and mix together and leave for 20 minutes, after remove the excess vinegar.
2. While waiting put 1 tablespoon of oil with the butter in a skillet and heat.
3. Place the pitta in and fry until golden this will take about 5 minutes.
4. Next add the almonds, keep cooking so the pitta becomes crunchy and the almonds toasted.
5. Take off the heat and add the chili flakes, salt and sumac, leave to cool.
6. When you are about to dish up mix the spinach with the pita in a bowl then stir in the date mix with the lemon juice and 1 tablespoon of oil.
7. Correct the seasoning and serve.

Fattoush

Prep time: 15 minutes
Cooking time: 10 minutes
Servings: 6 persons

Ingredients

- 1⅔ cups buttermilk
- 3 large tomatoes
- 1 tablespoon dried mint
- 1 ½ teaspoon salt
- 2 cloves garlic
- 2 scallions, sliced thin
- 3 small cucumbers, about 9 ounces, peeled and diced
- 3 tablespoons lemon juice
- 2 large flatbreads or naan
- ½ ounce fresh mint
- 2 tablespoons cider
- 1 tablespoon sumac
- ½ ounce flat leaf parsley, chopped
- ¼ cup olive oil
- 2 garlic cloves, crushed
- ¾ teaspoon black pepper

Directions

1. Rip the bread apart into edible pieces and place in a bowl.
2. Mix in the buttermilk along with the rest of the ingredients, stir it all together and allow to rest for 10 minutes.
3. Ladle into the serving bowls and sprinkle over some oil and finish with the sumac.

Jerusalem Falafel

Prep time: 80 minutes
Cooking time: 25 minutes
Servings: 6 persons

Ingredients

- ½ cup onion, diced fine
- 2 tablespoons cilantro, chopped
- ¼ teaspoon ground cardamom
- 1 ½ tablespoon all-purpose flour
- ¼ teaspoon cayenne
- ½ teaspoon baking powder
- 1 garlic clove, crushed
- 1 ¼ cups chickpeas
- ½ teaspoon ground cumin
- 3 tablespoons water
- ½ teaspoon ground coriander
- ½ teaspoon sesame seeds, for finishing
- ¼ teaspoon cardamom
- 3 cups oil for cooking

Directions

1. If the chickpeas need soaking, do this the night before.
2. Next add the chickpeas, parsley, cilantro, garlic and onion to a blender and pulse until it becomes well mixed but not too much mushy.
3. Now add the mix to a bowl and put in the spices, flour baking powder and water, stir together well until it becomes smooth.
4. Leave in the fridge for 60 minutes to rest.
5. When ready heat the oil in a deep sided skillet or pan, you want it around 2 inches deep.
6. Mold the mix into golf ball size and flatten out making them an oblong shape.
7. Dust with sesame seeds and deep fry them for 4-5 minutes, until golden brown.
8. Take out and place on kitchen paper to remove excess oil.
9. Dish up with lettuce and pitta bread.

Chicken with Cardamom Rice

Prep time: 15 minutes
Cooking time: 55 minutes
Servings: 6 persons

Ingredients

- 4 tablespoons olive oil
- 10 cardamom pods
- 3 tablespoons sugar
- 2 ¼ pounds chicken thighs, bone in and skin on
- 2 long cinnamon sticks, broken in 2
- 2 ½ tablespoons barberries or currants
- ¼ teaspoon cloves, whole
- 2 ¼ cups boiling water
- ¼ cup cilantro, chopped
- 2 medium onions, halved and sliced thin
- 1⅔ cups basmati rice
- Seasoning to taste
- ½ cup dill leaves, chopped
- 1/3 cup Greek yogurt mixed with 2 tablespoons of oil

Directions

1. Heat the sugar with barley, 3 tablespoons of water until it melts, take off the heat and put in the barberries and leave on the side.
2. While that is happening, add half the oil to a large skillet and heat, drop in the onions and fry for 6-7 minutes stir until golden, take out and place in a bowl.
3. Next the chicken to a bowl and dust with the seasoning, pour in the rest of the oil, cloves, cinnamon, and cardamom blend it all together well using your hands.
4. Place the chicken with the spices in the skillet and seal all over.
5. Now take out the chicken and don't worry about the spices they can stay there, remove any excess oil and add the rice with the onions and season, strain off the barberries and add them also.
6. Mix together and return the chicken, compressing it into the rice.
7. Ladle over the hot water place a lid on and cook for 30 minutes.
8. Once done take off and also take the lid off, now lay over the top a clean tea towel and replace the lid, leave on the side for 10 minutes.
9. Lastly add the herbs and blend them in, fluffing the rice at the same time, correct the seasoning and dish up with the yogurt.

Lemon and Leek Meatballs

Prep time: 40 minutes
Cooking time: 45 minutes
Servings: 3-4 persons

Ingredients

- 9 ounces ground beef
- 1 ¼ teaspoon salt
- 1 cup chicken stock
- 1 ¾ pound leeks trimmed and sliced
- 2 large eggs
- ⅓ cup fresh lemon juice
- 2 tablespoons of oil
- 1 teaspoon black pepper
- 1 cup bread crumbs
- ⅓ cup Greek yogurt, for serving
- 1 tablespoon parsley, chopped, for serving

Directions

1. Once the leeks are prepared, cook by steaming them for 15 – 20 minutes and drain when done, place on the side and squeeze dry.
2. When dry add to a bowl with the breadcrumbs, ground meat, seasoning and eggs mix together well, it is best done by hand.
3. Divide into 8 and shape into patties, then cool in the fridge.
4. After 25 minutes, heat the oil in a skillet and seal the meat until golden on both sides, you can place a lid on if desired.
5. Next place the stock in the pan until the patties are ¾ covered only, sprinkle over the lemon juice and cook by simmering for 30 minutes.
6. When done take off the lid and let down the stock until it has gone.
7. Take the skillet off the heat and rest on the side, to cool.
8. Dish the patties up warm with the yogurt and a dusting of parsley.

Roasted Chicken with Clementine
Prep time: 20 minutes
Cooking time: 45 minutes
Servings: 4 persons

Ingredients
- 3 tablespoons fresh orange juice
- 8 pieces of chicken drumsticks or thighs, skin on
- 3 tablespoons grain mustard
- 6 ½ tablespoons arak or pernod
- 2 teaspoons kosher salt
- 2 ½ teaspoons crushed fennel seeds
- 3 tablespoons light brown sugar
- Ground black pepper to taste
- 4 clementine's, peel on and sliced
- 3 tablespoons fresh lemon juice
- 3 medium onions, cut into 4
- Sprigs of fresh thyme
- ¼ cup olive oil

Directions
1. Prep heat the stove to 475°F.
2. Blend together the orange and lemon juice with the oil, mustard, arak and brown sugar in a bowl then season.
3. Lay the chicken with the skin side up into a roasting tray, add in the onion wedges, clementine's, thyme and fennel seeds, ladle over the sauce and using your hands mix together.
4. Place in the oven and cook for 30 minutes before reducing the heat to 400°F, you want the skin brown and crisp but not burnt, so watch it while cooking, it depends on your oven, after you have lowered the heat cook for a further 15 – 20 minutes.
5. Once done add the onion, clementine's and chicken to the platters and rest for 5-10 minutes.
6. Reduce the sauce if you desire it to be thicker, and ladle over the chicken, enjoy.

Cholent

Prep time: 20 minutes
Cooking time: 480 minutes
Servings: 6 persons

Ingredients

- 6 onions, peeled and diced or sliced
- 1 cup barley, soaked the night before
- 3 tablespoons canola oil or olive oil
- 5 potatoes, peeled and dice into large pieces
- 1 cup pinto beans, soaked over night
- ¾ of a chicken cut into 6 pieces
- 1 teaspoon paprika
- ½ teaspoon black pepper
- ¾ teaspoon salt
- 1 teaspoon garlic powder
- 1 teaspoon turmeric

Directions

1. Add the oil to a slow cooker, and fry the onions for 5-7 minutes.
2. Now put in the potatoes, beans and barley, add water to cover and leave it 2-3 inches from the top of the cooker.
3. Season and add all the spices along with the chicken.
4. Cook on a high setting for 4 hours, now check and correct the seasoning.
5. Now turn to low and cook until the following day.
6. Dish up and enjoy.

Chicken Skewers with Pearl Couscous Salad

Prep time: 30 minutes
Cooking time: 30 minutes
Servings: 6 persons

Ingredients

- 3 teaspoons ground cumin
- 1 teaspoon dried oregano
- 1 tablespoon sweet paprika
- ¼ cup olive oil
- 3 pound of chicken breasts, diced into cubes
- 1 teaspoon coriander
- For the salad
- 2 cups chicken stock
- 1 bunch fresh coriander
- 2 ½ cups pearl couscous
- 2 tablespoons olive oil
- 3 ripe tomatoes, but firm, and chopped
- 1 bunch fresh flat parsley, chopped
- 1 lemon, juiced
- ¼ pound labneh, or a soft cream cheese

Directions

1. Add a skillet to the stove and heat, once hot drop in the cumin, paprika, and cumin, toast these by stirring for 1 minute.
2. Once done place in a bowl and mix with the oil, 1 teaspoon of salt, chicken and oregano, mix well cover and rest in the fridge for 30 mins.
3. While waiting add 1 tablespoon of oil to a skillet and drop in the couscous brown this for 2 minutes, then add 1 cup of water with the stock and boil.
4. Turn down the heat place a lid on and cook for 15 minutes until soft.
5. Add the couscous to a dish, mix in the rest of the oil and allow to rest for 10 minutes.
6. Next mix in the coriander, juice, parsley and tomatoes season and put to one side for 30 minutes.
7. While waiting skewer the chicken and place on the barbecue are you can char grill them, cook for 10 minutes turning as you cook.
8. Add the couscous to the platters sprinkle with the cheese and place the chicken on top, enjoy.

Eggplants with Lamb and Pine nuts
Prep time: 35 minutes
Cooking time: 55 minutes
Servings: 4 persons

Ingredients
- 4 – 1 pound eggplants, slice in 2 from top to bottom
- 1 tablespoon ground cinnamon
- 2 teaspoons tomato paste
- 1 ½ teaspoons sweet paprika
- 1 tablespoon olive oil
- ¼ cup fresh parsley, chopped
- 1 teaspoon tamarind concentrate
- Ground pepper to taste
- 1-pound ground lamb
- 1 tablespoon sugar
- 1 large onion, finely chopped
- 1 ½ teaspoon ground cumin
- 1 tablespoon fresh lemon juice
- Salt to taste
- 3 tablespoons pine nuts
- 1 – 1 ½ inch cinnamon stick

Directions
1. Heat the stove to 425°.
2. Lay out the eggplants on a baking tray with the sliced side up and smear with oil and seasoning, cook for 18-22 minutes until golden.
3. Blend together the paprika, cinnamon and cumin in a bowl.
4. Add 1 tablespoon of oil to a frying pan and fry the onions for 6-7minutes, now mix in the lamb and fry for 4 minutes breaking it up.
5. Once cook remove the excess fat, but leave 1 tablespoon inside.
6. Mix in the tomato paste, nuts, 1 teaspoon of sugar and half of the parsley, season.
7. Ladle the meat mix on top of the eggplants.
8. Blend together using a small dish the rest of the spices with ½ cup water, sugar, lemon juice, seasoning and tamarind.
9. Add this mix to the baking tray put in the cinnamon stick, cover with foil and cook for 50 minutes.
10. While cooking baste once or twice to give more flavor.
11. Add the eggplants to the platters, take out the stick and ladle over the juices, dust with parsley.

Shrimp Harissa Tagine
Prep time: 15 minutes
Cooking time: 20 minutes
Servings: 2 persons

Ingredients
- ½ cup of water
- 1 tablespoon fresh parsley
- 31-40 frozen shrimp
- ⅓ cup yellow onion, chopped fine
- 1 packet saffron simmer sauce
- 1 tablespoon garlic, minced
- 1 tablespoon fresh cilantro, chopped roughly
- 2 cups pearl couscous, cooked
- ½ teaspoon seas salt
- 2 tablespoon oil
- 1 tablespoon spice mix

Directions
1. Heat the stove to 400°F.
2. Cook the shrimps in boiling water for 6 minutes over a high heat.
3. Take off and drain if they have shells remove them.
4. Now add them to an oven proof bowl with the water, spice, seasoning, cilantro, parsley, garlic and salt.
5. Next spoon over the sauce and sprinkle oil over the top.
6. Cook in the oven for 20 minutes.
7. While waiting cook the couscous on top of the stove.
8. Take out the shrimps and place a lid over the top, allow them to steam.
9. After 6-8 minutes dish up with the couscous on a platter.

Side Dishes

Green Couscous

Prep time: 25 minutes
Cooking time: 10 minutes
Servings: 4 persons

Ingredients

- ¾ cup boiling water or vegetable stock
- ¼ teaspoon salt
- 1 cup couscous
- 1 tablespoon olive oil
- ¼ teaspoon ground cumin
- 1 small onion, sliced thin
- For the herb paste
- 1 cup cilantro chopped
- 2 tablespoons dill chopped
- 3 scallions, sliced fine
- 3 tablespoons olive oil, more if needed
- ⅓ cup parsley chopped
- 2 tablespoons mint, chopped
- 1 fresh green chili, chopped
- 2 tablespoons tarragon
- 1 ¼ cup arugula leaves, chopped

Directions

1. Add the couscous to a bowl and place the water over, put cling wrap over the bowl and leave it on the side for 10 minutes.
2. While waiting add the oil to a skillet and cook the onions for 7 minutes until golden, season and add the cumin.
3. Next add all the herb ingredients to a blender and pulse until smooth.
4. Mix in the paste into the couscous.
5. Now add the onions, chili, arugula and scallions fold in and serve.

Israeli cauliflower

Prep time: 40 minutes
Cooking time: 30 minutes
Servings: 4-6 persons

Ingredients

- For the vinaigrette
- 2 tablespoons honey
- 2 teaspoons kosher salt
- ¼ cup wine vinegar
- 3 tablespoons virgin olive oil
- 1 teaspoon Dijon mustard
- Pinch black pepper
- For the cauliflower
- 1 cup all-purpose flour
- 1 teaspoon ground black pepper
- 1 large head cauliflower, cut into florets
- 5 cups canola oil
- 1 teaspoon ground pink pepper
- 3 teaspoons kosher salt

To finish
- Toasted pine nuts
- Chopped parsley
- Dried currants

Directions

1. To make the vinaigrette, beat together the honey, mustard and vinegar.
2. Now add slowly the oil and keep beating.
3. Finish with the seasoning and place on one side.
4. Add water to a pan and boil, and heat the oil in a thick based pan.
5. Add the cauliflower to the water for 2 minutes to blanch them, then refresh to stop them cooking under cold water.
6. Mix the salt, peppers and flour together, then dip the cauliflower in the mix, until coated.
7. Fry the cauliflower for 4-5 minutes in the hot oil and drain when done on kitchen paper.
8. To serve place the cauliflower on the platter and sprinkle over the vinaigrette.
9. Finish with the nuts, currants and parsley on top.

Potato Salad

Prep time: 10 minutes
Cooking time: 25 minutes
Servings: 2-3 persons

Ingredients

- ½ pound potatoes, peeled
- 1 teaspoon dried mint
- 1 tablespoon olive oil
- ⅛ teaspoon salt
- 1 tablespoon vinegar
- ⅛ teaspoon black pepper
- 1 medium onion, halved and sliced

Directions

1. Cut the potatoes into cubes about 1 inch × 1 inch.
2. Cook in salted water for 20 minutes until just tender.
3. Add these to the serving dish.
4. Gently blend in the seasoning, vinegar, oil, mint and onions.
5. When mix together, place in the fridge to cool until ready to serve.

Butternut Squash and Tahini Spread

Prep time: 15 minutes
Cooking Time: 70 minutes
Servings: 6-8 persons

Ingredients

- 3 tablespoons olive oil
- ¼ cup tahini paste
- 1 large butternut squash, peeled and diced
- ½ teaspoon salt
- 1 ½ teaspoon date syrup
- 2 small garlic cloves, crushed
- 1 teaspoon ground cinnamon
- ½ cup Greek yogurt
- 2 tablespoons coriander, chopped
- 1 teaspoon mixed black and white sesame seeds, or white only

Directions

1. Heat the stove to 350°F.
2. Lay out the squash onto a baking sheet and sprinkle oil, salt and cinnamon over the top, blend together, then using baking foil cover the top and wrap tight, cook for 70 minutes, mixing once during the cooking time, take out and rest when done.
3. Once it has cooled down place into a blender with the garlic, tahini and yogurt, pulse until it becomes a rough paste, not smooth.
4. Dish up smeared over a platter with sesame seeds, coriander and syrup drizzled over the top.

Roasted Jerusalem Artichokes

Prep time: 10 minutes
Cooking time: 35 minutes
Servings: 4 persons

Ingredients

- 2 tablespoons dried thyme
- Sea salt to taste
- 1 pound artichokes, Jerusalem
- 1 tablespoon garlic, minced
- ¾ cup olive oil

Directions

1. Heat the stove to 350°F.
2. Wash and scrub the artichokes and remove the eyes, slice into 1 inch lengths.
3. Add the garlic, oil, salt and thyme together in a large dish.
4. Now mix in the artichokes and mix together.
5. Lay out on a baking tray and cook for 35-45 minutes.
6. Dish up when ready.

Potato Kugel with Fried Shallots

Prep time: 45 minutes
Cooking time: 75 minutes
Servings: 10 persons

Ingredients

- 4 large shallots
- ⅓ cup potato starch
- ½ teaspoon fresh ground pepper
- 1 cup vegetable oil
- 1 large yellow onion, roughly grated
- 5 large eggs, beaten
- ⅓ cup potato starch
- 5 pounds Idaho potatoes, peeled and grated
- ½ cup extra virgin olive oil
- 1 tablespoon kosher salt
- 2 large egg yolks, beaten
- 1 cup boiling water

Directions

1. Heat the stove 450°F.
2. Add the vegetables and heat, fry the onions for about 5 minutes once golden take out and put to one side on a platter, keeping the oil.
3. Squeeze the potatoes dry and place into a large dish, now mix in the seasoning, potato starch, onions and nutmeg, mix well.
4. Next add the 2 types of egg, boiling water and olive oil, stir and add the onions, mix well.
5. Add two ceramic dishes to the stove and heat, or two cast iron dishes.
6. Put in each dish 2 tablespoons of the shallot oil, once it begins to smoke add the potato mix evenly spreading it out.
7. Now place them in the oven and cook for 20 minutes, reduce the heat to 375°F and cook for a further 40 minutes until golden.
8. Heat the broiler and grill the potatoes near the top for 2 minutes to crisp them up.
9. Take out and cool, after about 20 minutes slice into squares and dish up.

Avocado Toast with Tahini Rosewater

Prep time: 10 minutes
Cooking time: 5 minutes
Servings: 2 persons

Ingredients

- 2 slices rye bread, toasted
- ½ teaspoon rosewater
- ¼ cup tahini paste
- 2 eggs, fried
- 1 tablespoon honey
- Olive oil, for garnish
- Sea salt, to taste
- ½ avocado, sliced
- Sesame seed, for garnish

Directions

1. Blend together the rosewater, honey and tahini in a bowl.
2. Smear the mix over the roast and place the sliced avocado on top.
3. Add the egg to the top of the avocado and finish with the seeds and salt, sprinkle over a little olive oil.
4. Enjoy.

Chickpea Sephardic Salad with Grilled Eggplant

Prep time: 15 minutes
Cooking time: 10 minutes
Servings: 4 persons

Ingredients

- 2 tablespoons extra virgin olive oil
- 1 large eggplant
- Finely chopped mint, for garnish
- 1 – 16ounce can chickpeas, drained and washed
- Salt to taste
- 2 tablespoons pitted black olives
- 3 Roma tomatoes, diced
- For the dressing
- ¼ teaspoon cumin
- 1 tablespoon white vinegar
- 2 cloves garlic, minced
- Salt to taste
- ¼ teaspoon black pepper
- ½ teaspoon paprika
- ⅓ cup virgin olive oil
- Pita chips to serve with

Directions

1. Cut the eggplant into slices and dust with set, let them rest for 30 minutes to take out the water and bitterness, then rinse, dry with kitchen paper.
2. Heat a pan or heat the grill.
3. Sprinkle oil over the eggplant and grill for 4-5 minutes on each side, cool and dice.
4. Mix together the chickpeas, eggplant, tomatoes and olives in a bowl, then place on the side.
5. Using another bowl, mix together the ingredients for the dressing apart from the salt and oil.
6. Now blend in the oil slowly while beating and add the seasoning.
7. Mix the salad with the dressing and dish up with the chips.

Shabbat Salad

Prep time: 15 minutes
Cooking time: 25 minutes
Servings: 4 persons

Ingredients

- 1 bunch asparagus, trimmed, washed and dried
- 2 cloves garlic, minced
- ¼ cup dried cranberries
- Seasoning to taste
- 4 cups arugula
- ½ cup carrots, cut into thin strips
- 2 cups red potatoes, washed and cut into 4
- 2 cups challah bread, stale and diced into cubes
- 1 cup chicken, shredded
- Olive oil for drizzling
- For the dressing
- 1 teaspoon Dijon mustard
- 2 tablespoons red wine vinegar
- ⅓ cup olive oil
- Seasoning
- 1 clove garlic, minced

Directions

1. Heat the stove to 400°F.
2. Trim the asparagus and place on a baking tray with the potato quarters, sprinkle oil and seasoning over the top and cook for 25 minutes.
3. Meanwhile fry the diced bread with the garlic for the croutons, or they can be placed in the oven also for 10 minutes.
4. While they are cooking, add the mustard, minced garlic, lemon juice and vinegar together in a bowl, mix together.
5. Next slowly beat in the oil and season.
6. Place ¾ of the dressing over the arugula and put the potatoes on top with the carrots, asparagus, croutons, chicken and cranberries.
7. Finish with the rest of the croutons over the top.

Brussel Sprouts with Gribenes

Prep time: 10 minutes
Cooking time: 20 minutes
Servings: 4-6 persons

Ingredients

- 1 pound Brussel sprouts, washed, trimmed and halved
- ¼ teaspoon black pepper
- ¼ cup chopped pecans
- ½ teaspoon kosher salt
- 1 ½ extra virgin olive oil
- Balsamic vinegar to drizzle

Directions

1. Heat the stove to 400°F.
2. Lay out the pecans on a baking tray and roast until golden this will be quick so keep an eye on them, you do not want them burnt.
3. Place the cleaned sprouts into a bowl and mix with the olive oil and season.
4. Lay out on the baking tray covered in foil and cook for 20 minutes, turn over half way, cook until dark golden.
5. Mix with the pecan mix in a bowl, sprinkle over the vinegar and dish up while hot.

Matbucha

Prep time: 20 minutes
Cooking time: 120 minutes
Servings: 4 persons

Ingredients

- 1-pound red bell peppers
- 1 ½ teaspoons hot paprika
- 2 pounds' tomatoes
- 3 cloves garlic, cut into 4
- 1 teaspoon salt
- 3 dried chilies
- ⅓ cup olive oil

Directions

1. Heat the stove to 350°F.
2. Place the peppers on a baking tray and cook to brown the skins.
3. Meanwhile cross the top of the tomatoes and blanch in boiling water for 30 seconds, take out and remove the skins.
4. Halve the tomatoes and remove the seeds and juice, now dice them.
5. Take the skins of the peppers and also dice.
6. Next add the entire ingredients to a pot and put the oil over the top.
7. Heat until it boils, then reduce the heat and cook with a lid on for 2 hours.
8. Now take off the lid and cook until it becomes thick, stir so it does not burn.
9. Cool and serve or put in the fridge until you are ready.

Snacks

Lamb and Bulgur Wheat Croquettes

Prep time: 15 minutes
Cooking time: 10 minutes
Servings: 6-8 persons

Ingredients

- For the shell
- 1 teaspoon kosher salt
- ½ teaspoon ground coriander
- 1-pound ground lamb
- 1 small yellow onion, minced
- 1 ¼ cups fine bulgur wheat, soaked for 10 minutes in warm water
- Black pepper to taste
- For the filling
- 1 large yellow onion, minced
- 2 teaspoon ground all spice
- 2 tablespoons olive oil
- ⅓ cup toasted pine nuts
- 3 cloves garlic, minced
- 8 ounces ground chuck
- Canola oil for frying
- 2 teaspoons cinnamon
- Kosher salt and black pepper to taste

Directions

1. Using a blender add the lamb, cumin, onion, seasoning, coriander, and wheat, pulse until it becomes a paste, then put to one side.
2. Clean the blender and add the filling ingredients pulse these together until it is smooth.
3. Next take 2 tablespoons of the shell mix and roll or compress into flat rounds about 3 inches wide.
4. Add 1 tablespoon of the filling to the center and fold up the sides to form balls, repeat until the mix has finished.
5. Add 2 inches of oil to a pan and heat.
6. Once hot fry for 4-8 minutes until golden and cooked through.
7. Dish up.

Fried Artichokes

Prep time: 25 minutes
Cooking time: 15 minutes
Servings: 4 persons

Ingredients

- 12 baby artichokes
- 3 lemons, divided
- Olive oil for cooking

Directions

1. Slice 1 of the lemons in 2 and squeeze the juice into a bowl, big enough to take all the artichokes, add water until the bowl is 2/3rd full.
2. Remove the leaves from the artichoke until you come to the pale green ones then cut the stalk and remove ½ inch from the top.
3. In another bowl put water with ice.
4. Drop the artichokes in a pot of boiling water with salt for 10 seconds, and transfer to the ice water.
5. Once cool take out and drain put on kitchen paper upside down and press down so the leaves open up.
6. Next put 2 inches of oil in a pan and heat, cook one artichoke at a time in the oil holding it down with tongs for 15 seconds.
7. Now let it go and it will turn around and let it cook until it becomes soft, this will take around 4 more minutes.
8. Repeat until they are all cooked.
9. Dust with salt and serve with the lemon wedges.

Flatbreads with Mushroom, Ricotta and Herbs

Prep time: 35 minutes
Cooking time: 10 minutes
Servings: 12 persons

Ingredients

- 1 shallot, minced
- ¼ cup extra virgin olive oil
- ¼ cup dry white wine
- 1 cup ricotta cheese
- ½ pound oyster and shiitake mushrooms, sliced
- Seasoning to taste
- 2 tablespoons chervil, chopped
- 2 tablespoons tarragon, chopped
- 1 clove garlic, minced
- 2 tablespoons flat leaf parsley, chopped
- 2 – 8ounce balls pizza dough
- 2 tablespoons chives, chopped

Directions

1. Add ¼ cup of oil to frying pan and heat.
2. When hot fry the mushrooms for 5 minutes then add in the garlic with the shallot for a further 1 minute.
3. Next add the wine, season and cook for another 1 minute.
4. Grease a flat baking tray and light the grill or use a griddle pan on the stove top, mold the dough balls into 12-inch pizza bases and smear with oil.
5. Cook for 2 minutes, but do not burn, then turn them over and put on the cheese, herbs and mushrooms, cooking for a further 2 minutes.
6. Take off the heat, sprinkle over some olive oil and season.
7. Slice and dish up.

Jaffa Cakes

Prep time: 10 minutes
Cooking time: 10 minutes
Servings: 12 cakes

Ingredients

For the cake:
- 2 eggs, room temperature
- ¼ cup sugar
- ¼ cup all-purpose flour

For the filling:
- 1 3-ounce box jello mix
- 1 tablespoon orange marmalade
- ½ cup boiling water
- 8 ounces dark chocolate
-

Directions
1. Preheat over to 350°F.
2. In a bowl, combine jello mix and boiling water and stir until completely dissolved.
3. Add orange marmalade and stir until fully incorporated.
4. Pour this mixture into a 9x13 dish and refrigerate for at least four hours.
5. In a mixer, whip eggs and sugar until pale and fluffy – about 4-5 minutes.
6. Slowly add flour while continuing to beat egg mixture
7. Pour batter into the bottom of a 12-hole non-stick muffin tin, or heavily greased and floured regular tin.
8. Bake in oven 8-10 minutes. Remove and cool slightly before removing cakes. Let cool on cooling racks.
9. Melt chocolate for 30 seconds on high power in the microwave.
10. Remove jello mixture. Spread a small scoop of the jello mixture on each of the 12 cakes. When done, cover with the melted chocolate.
11. Let the chocolate harden and then enjoy!

Tomato and Egg (Shakshooka)

Prep time: 10 minutes
Cooking time: 35 minutes
Servings: 6 persons

Ingredients

- 3 cloves garlic
- Salt to taste
- 5 ripe tomatoes
- 6 eggs
- 2 tablespoons oil for cooking
- 1 medium onion
- Red pepper to taste
- ½ large green pepper

Directions

1. Dice the tomatoes and cut the peppers into strips, then place together in a bowl.
2. Dice the onion and garlic finely.
3. Add the oil to a skillet and fry the garlic with the onion for 5 minutes.
4. Reduce the heat and put in the peppers and tomatoes with the red pepper and salt.
5. Place a lid on and cook until the tomatoes are tender.
6. Crack the eggs over the vegetables, re-cover and cook for another 10 minutes.
7. Place onto a platter and dish up.

Fava Bean Salad

Prep time: 5 minutes
Cooking time: 10 minutes
Servings: 4 persons

Ingredients

- 1 tablespoon olive oil
- ½ teaspoon black pepper
- 1 can fava beans, drained
- 1 tablespoon lemon juice
- ½ teaspoon salt
- Pitta bread ripped to serve

Directions

1. Drain off the bean juice and place in a pan.
2. Put on the stove and heat and mash them, either with a potato masher or spoon, cook until they are thick and hot through.
3. Mix in the lemon juice seasoning to taste and the oil.
4. Dish up with the broken pitta pieces.

Desserts

Knafeh with Walnuts

Prep time: 30 minutes
Cooking time: 40 minutes
Servings: persons

Ingredients

- ½ cup butter, dissolved
- 1 pound walnuts, chopped
- 1 tablespoon cinnamon
- For the dough
- 1 cup sugar
- 3 cups semolina
- 1 cup ghee
- For the syrup
- ½ teaspoon rose water
- 6 cups sugar
- ½ teaspoon lemon juice

Directions

1. Make the syrup by adding the lemon juice, rosewater, sugar and 2 cups of water to a pan and bring to the boil, whisking all the time, once it boils turn the heat down and keep cooking for a further 5 minutes, put to one side.
2. Blend the cinnamon with the walnuts in a separate container.
3. To make the dough, blend together the 3 ingredients and ¼ cup of water, lay on a baking tray and cook for 5 minutes in the oven, but do not color.
4. When it cools knock it back with your hands.
5. Mix in the butter and blend together well this will take about 15 minutes.
6. Cut the dough into 2, lay one halve on the baking tray then sprinkle over the walnuts, add the other halve of the dough to the top.
7. Bake in the oven for 30 minutes once golden take out and remove from the tray.
8. Ladle over the syrup straight away.
9. Dish up hot.

Israeli Fruit Cup

Prep time: 15 minutes
Cooking time: 0 minutes
Servings: 10 persons

Ingredients

- 4 large bananas
- 5 figs, dried
- ⅔ cup red wine, sweet
- 8 navel oranges
- 2 oranges, juiced
- Sugar to taste
- ½ cup walnuts, chopped
- 1 cup raisins

Directions

1. Take the oranges and peel them, cut segment and remove any pith, and dice roughly.
2. Using a bowl dice the figs and mix together with the diced oranges.
3. Now cut the bananas into slices and add.
4. Next put in the orange juice and mix, followed by the walnuts, raisins and wine.
5. Finally add the sugar if needed, taste first.
6. Dish up.

Chocolate Torte with Macerated Strawberries

Prep time: 20 minutes
Cooking time: 25 minutes
Servings: 8-10 persons

Ingredients

- 6 tablespoons brown sugar
- 6 eggs
- 2 tablespoons instant expresso powder
- 6 tablespoons white sugar
- 10 ounces dark chocolate, chopped
- 3 tablespoons icing sugar
- 8 ounces' strawberries, sliced
- 1 cup heavy cream, whipped
- Icing sugar to dust at the finish

Directions

1. Heat the stove to 350°F and spray grease, then line a cake tin.
2. Beat the eggs together with the sugars, until it becomes fluffy and light.
3. Dissolve the chocolate over stream not on direct heat, then gradually add to the eggs whisking all the time.
4. Next mix in the expresso.
5. Pour the mix into the cake tin and cook for around 25 minutes.
6. Once it is firm and has risen take out and rest in the tin.
7. Do not worry it will sink in the center.
8. Now blend together the icing sugar with the strawberries and rest them for 30 minutes.
9. To dish up cut the cake and place on the platter with some cream and the strawberries.
10. Sprinkle over some icing sugar to finish.

Apple Cake
Prep time: 20 minutes
Cooking time: 90 minutes
Servings: 6-8 persons

Ingredients
- 1 tablespoon ground cinnamon
- 6 apples
- 5 tablespoons granulated sugar
- For the cake
- 1 tablespoon baking powder
- ¼ cup orange juice
- 2 ¾ cups flour
- 4 large eggs
- 1 teaspoon fine seas salt
- 2 ½ teaspoons vanilla extract
- 1 cup vegetable oil
- 2 cups granulated sugar

Directions
1. Heat the stove to 350°F and grease the cake tin.
2. Take the apples and core and peel them before cutting them into cubes, now mix the cubes with 5 tablespoons of sugar and the cinnamon, place on one side.
3. Next blend the flour with the salt and baking powder using a large dish.
4. Using a different dish mix together the orange juice, eggs, sugar, oil and vanilla beat well.
5. Add this to the flour and mix well.
6. Place half of the mix in the cake tin, followed by half of the apples, including any juice.
7. Repeat the process with the remaining ingredients and arrange the apples over the top.
8. Cook for 90 minutes, before removing from the oven, test the center with a knife to see if it comes out clean.
9. If you find it is coloring too fast, cover with foil to stop it burning.
10. Dish up when ready or even keep for the following day.

Easy Cheesecake

Prep time: 10 minutes
Cooking time: 10 minutes
Servings: 4 persons

Ingredients

- 2 cups full fat milk
- 1 packet plain tea biscuits
- 1 packet kosher instant strawberry gelatin
- 1 – 8-ounce container cream cheese
- 1 packet instant vanilla pudding

Directions

1. Powder the biscuits and leave on one side.
2. Mix the milk, cheese and pudding powder together and keep on the side.
3. Next make the gelatin to the directions on the packet and cool.
4. Take the serving glasses and add some of the crumb mix in the base then put a layer of the cheese mix.
5. Repeat this with a second layer and put in the fridge to cool.
6. Add the gelatin to the top just before it sets and put back in the fridge.
7. When set, serve.

Apple Berry Cobblers

Prep time: 15 minutes
Cooking time: 40 minutes
Servings: 2 persons

Ingredients

- ½ teaspoon almond extract
- ⅓ cup blueberries
- ½ cup water
- 2 teaspoons sweetener, if required
- 1 small apple, peeled and diced
- 1 fresh almond biscotti

Directions

1. Heat the stove to 350°F.
2. Add the water to a dish and drop in the almond extract.
3. Run the biscuit through the water fast and keep on the side.
4. Now mix together the blueberries, sugar and apple.
5. Place the mix into 1 large or 2 smaller ramekins.
6. Hold the biscuit over the top and crush it to cover the top.
7. Cook in the oven for 40 minutes.
8. Dish up when ready.

Doughnuts with Raisins and Pine Nuts

Prep time: 120 minutes
Cooking time: 15 minutes
Servings: 32 persons

Ingredients

- ½ teaspoon sugar
- ¼ cup raisins
- 1 ½ cups warm water, divided
- ¼ cup pine nuts
- 1 ½ cups honey
- 1 envelope active dried yeast
- 1 large egg, beaten
- ¾ cup water
- ½ teaspoon salt
- 3 cup all-purpose flour
- 1 tablespoon vegetable oil, plus extra for cooking

Directions

1. Blend together the ¼ cup of warm water with the sugar in a dish and dust with the yeast, stir and allow to rest for 5 minutes.
2. Mix together the flour with the salt in a separate large dish,
3. Now create a well in the middle and add the pine nuts, egg, raisins and 1 tablespoon of oil, then add the rest of the warm water and top that with the yeast water, mix all together into a dough.
4. Cover with a cloth and rest for 90 minutes to expand in size.
5. Next add kitchen paper to a large baking tray and put on the side.
6. Heat the oil for cooking in a deep pan, you need around 2 inches of oil in the pan, if you have a thermometer bring up to 365°F.
7. Now fry the doughnuts, scooping out 1 tablespoon of the dough at a time, and cook in sets of 6 for around 5 minutes until golden, turning over half way.
8. Once done place on the prepared baking tray.
9. Using a pan beat the honey, cinnamon and ¾ cup water together, once it boils take the pan off the stove, dip in the doughnuts and put onto the serving platter.
10. Any spare syrup add to a bowl and serve on the side.

Sweet Honey Cake

Prep time: 20 minutes
Cooking time: 50 minutes
Servings: 20 persons

Ingredients

- 1 tablespoon baking powder
- 1 tablespoon cinnamon
- 1 cup apple sauce
- 2 ½ cups whole wheat flour or spelt
- ½ teaspoon ground cloves or allspice
- ½ cup sunflower oil
- ¼ cup sliced almonds
- 2 teaspoons baking soda
- 2 teaspoons vanilla extract
- ½ teaspoon ground ginger
- 1 cup pure maple syrup or dark agave nectar
- ½ cup golden raisins

Directions

1. Heat the stove to 325°F.
2. Blend together in a bowl the flour, baking soda and powder, ginger, cinnamon and cloves, then make a well in the middle.
3. Now add to the middle all the wet ingredients and mix in the raisins, keep the almonds on one side.
4. Once well mixed, add some parchment paper in the base of 2 loaf tins and grease the sides.
5. Add the mix to the 2 tins and dust over the top with the almonds.
6. Cook for 40 to 50 minutes in the oven, test with a knife and make sure it comes out clean.
7. Remove from the oven and cool.
8. Once cool ease the sides with a knife and take out then place onto a platter.
9. Slice and enjoy.

Nut Filled Pastry, Baklava

Prep time: 45 minutes
Cooking time: 25 minutes
Servings: 36 persons

Ingredients

- 1 ½ cups water
- 2 tablespoons light corn syrup
- 2 cinnamon sticks
- 3 cups sugar
- 2 tablespoons lemon juice
- For the filling
- ¼ cup sugar
- 1 pound of mixed pistachios, almonds and walnuts, ground or chopped fine
- ¼ teaspoon ground cloves
- 1-pound phyllo pastry
- 1 ½ teaspoons ground cinnamon
- 1 cup butter, dissolved

Directions

1. First make the syrup by, adding the lemon juice, corn syrup, water, cinnamon sticks and sugar to a pan and heat cook for 5 minutes to melt the sugar, then turn up the heat and cook for a further 5 minutes to make the syrup, remove the cinnamon sticks and cool.
2. Add the entire filling ingredients together and mix well, put to one side.
3. Heat the stove to 350°F.
4. Take a jelly roll pan or baking tray and spray grease.
5. Add 1 sheet of the pastry and smear butter over it, do this with 7 more sheets on top of each other.
6. Now smear over half of the filling and repeat with 8 more sheets of pastry on top with the butter between each other.
7. Trim up the edges with a sharp knife, then slice it into long strips roughly 1 ¾ inches wide only through the top layer, next cut 1 ½ inch wide the opposite way, making it look like diamonds.
8. Drizzle a little cold water over the top just before you bake.
9. Cook for 20 minutes in the oven, then turn the heat down and cook for a further 15 minutes or until it become golden.
10. Take out and slice through the lines already marked, and ladle over the syrup to soak in, cool completely before serving.

Chocolate, Cinnamon and Cayenne Macaroons

Prep time: 15 minutes
Cooking time: 25 minutes
Servings: 10 persons

Ingredients

- 1 cup sweetened condensed milk, 12-ounce can
- ½ teaspoon ground cinnamon
- ¼ teaspoon kosher salt
- 1 teaspoon pure vanilla extract
- 2 large egg whites
- 4 ounces dark chocolate, dissolved
- 4 ½ cups sweetened shredded coconut, 14-ounce can
- ½ teaspoon cayenne pepper

Directions

1. Heat the stove to 350°F, and put the shelves at the top and lower thirds of the stove, now line 2 baking trays.
2. Next blend together in a bowl, the vanilla, milk, coconut and cinnamon, mix well.
3. Whisk the whites with the salt until they form peaks, then gently mix into the coconut mix.
4. Make the mix into balls, this can be done using either wet hands or using 2 tablespoons, then place on the baking trays leaving a gap in between each.
5. Cook in the oven and while cooking change the trays around to cook even and color even this will take around 25 minutes.
6. Take out and rest on a wire rack.
7. Now take the chocolate and mix in the cayenne.
8. Spoon the chocolate over the top using a spoon at a distance from them, to from lines over them.

Apricot Hamantaschen
Prep time: 60 minutes
Cooking time: 25 minutes
Servings: 15 persons

Ingredients
- 4 large eggs
- 1 teaspoon fresh grated lemon zest
- 4 cups dried apricots or fresh
- ¾ cup walnuts, chopped
- 1 teaspoon fresh orange zest, grated
- 3 ½ cups all-purpose flour
- 1 ½ teaspoons baking powder
- 1 ½ cups granulated sugar

Directions
1. If using dried apricots, soak them in a bowl for 1 hour in boiling water.
2. Meanwhile, blend together the baking powder and flour.
3. Beat together 2 of the eggs, orange and lemon zest, and 1 cup of sugar, beat until the sugar has melted and the mix becomes creamy.
4. Now add the flour into the wet mix until you have a dough, cling wrap the dough and place in the fridge for 60 minutes.
5. If you soaked the apricots, strain off the water and dry on kitchen paper, then dice them and add to the walnuts with the rest of the sugar in a separate bowl.
6. Heat the stove to 350°F, and grease 2 baking trays.
7. Place the dough on a floured surface and roll until it becomes ¼ inch thick.
8. Now take a round cutter and press out 3 inch rounds.
9. Next add a tablespoon of the filling to each one, now fold up the edges and squeeze the joins together, but in the middle at the top, leave this open.
10. Collect the scraps of dough and re-roll them until it has all been used.
11. Lay out the finished ones on the baking tray, leave slight gaps between them.
12. Beat the last 2 eggs with 6 tablespoons of water and egg wash the dough, place in the oven and cook for 20-25 minutes, until golden.
13. Take out, cool and serve.

Encore Book Club

Fabulous Free eBook Cookbooks Every Week!

Our eBooks are FREE for the first few days of most publications. You will be the first to know when new books are published. We frequently offer exclusive promotions. Our collection includes hundreds of books that on a wide variety of topics including healthy foods, diets, food allergy alternatives, gourmet meals, desserts, and easy and inexpensive meals.

Sign-up at:
www.encorebookclub.com

**View a complete list of our
Best Selling Recipe Book Series:**
www.encorebookclub.com/booklist

Thank You for Your Purchase!

We know you have many choices when it comes to ready and recipe books. Your patronage is sincerely appreciated. If you would like to provide us feedback, go to www.encorebookclub.com/feedback.

Please Consider Writing an Amazon Review!

Happy with this book? If so, please consider writing a positive review. It helps others know it's a quality book and allows us to continue to promote our positive message. To writing reviews, go to http://geni.us/productreviews. Thank You!

Printed in Great Britain
by Amazon